WHEN STARS EXPLODE

WHEN STARS EXPLODE

Selected Poems
2002

HARRY P. KROITOR

Heron Press
2002

Library of Congress Cataloging-in-Publication Data

Kroitor, Harry P., 1924-
  When stars explode : selected poems / Harry P. Kroitor.
      p. cm.
  ISBN 0-9649764-3-9
  I. Title.
  PS3611.R64 W47 2002
  811'.54—dc21

                                              2002007420

Copyright © 2003 Harry P. Kroitor
Manufactured in the United States of America

ISBN 0-9649764-3-9

Contents

Acknowledgements
The following poems have previously appeared in *Perspectives in Biology and Medicine*, published by the University of Chicago Press and The Johns Hopkins University Press: *Limbic Lobe, Savage Gutturals, Rampant Genes, Yardsticks, Mind Into Matter, The Hamster and the Rat, African Genesis, Time Trap, The Mind's Scale, Mind Escape (Metamorphosis)), Unspliced Nerves, Past Ourselves, Free Creations. A Rose Is not a Name* was originally printed in *ETC: A Review of General Semantics*, Vol. XXIII, No. 3., International Society for General Semantics, Concord, California.

I
WHEN STARS EXPLODE

NOVA

Beyond the countless masks of god
Are countless masks that men create
Of all their fallen spires.

Nor ark nor babel nor lost Bacchus
Nor all our eastern minarets
Can equivocate
When universal time
Remembers to create of us a star—
When all our laws disintegrate in deepest space
Where only cosmic dust and light years are.

FREE CREATIONS

The place beyond our stars is crowded thought,
Filled with m-c squares and quiet visions,
With fusions, formulas, and mental fissions.

Incredible spiral nebulae, space-dust,
Red giants and white dwarfs play
Across uncharted thoughts in minds
Exploding with uncharted universes—
Quite at odds with the straightjackets
Of each earth-tied day.

MIND INTO MATTER

Riddler and riddle
Upstairs and outside
Energy and matter
Observer and observed
I and it
I.

"Seeing is learned,"
The psychologist asserted.
"At first you see things
Only upside down.
It's later that you make things Right."

"So I create all creatures—
Even geographic features—
In a universe uniquely mine?
And do I only will the line
That separates my world and yours?"

Certainty and probability.

Einstein, Heisenberg, and Emc^2
Energetic thought and matter paired.
It is our dreams create the world,
Its inconsistencies, dimensions,
Boundaries, and national pretensions.

"We are such stuff," the poet said.

And our universe hangs by a self-willed thread?

IMPRINT OF LIGHT YEARS

Shadows are the sun's way
Of smiting man through universes—
Imprinting light years on a moment
Filled with twice too many certainties.

Sighs are the soul's breath—
Radioactive in atomic times—
The firebrand of inner heat and heart
On all of our uncertainties.

Sr90

I have seen your smog-choked cities,
seen their faces begging pities,
seen their blighted hearts in stone decay—
and I learned dismay.

I have raced down tarred and paved roads,
cursed a thousand cars of grave-loads
flying toward their worm-eternity
till my flesh felt gritty.

I've walked through a thousand grey-minds,
seen too many uncreative yea-kinds
cowing hope into mass submission—
and so I sought the last physician.

I have seen your radioactive clouds,
seen them wrap the world in radioactive shrouds,
till the Sr90 by the jet-winds blown
taught me cancer of the bone.

YARDSTICKS

To measure ordinary days
Requires stars—
The firelight of years
Across some finite, starless space.

But how to gauge this day of ours?

The yardstick of the stars
Will not suffice
For motions of the heart—
Its heat, its ice—
For these, the measure of the mind
And half of our eternity will do.

Will do, perhaps, to start.

WORLDS IN COLLISION

Master ant and butterfly,
ape and lava, hot stars in black skies,
before condemning neighbors' deviant lies.

Man and poetry both lie their way
to meaning and to fragmentary truth,
proclaiming gods and molecules en route.

The lightning heel of Elohim,
the final cosmic chill, begins within,
where we with worlds in collision spin.

TIME TRAP

If we measure human time
In windblown thistles
And bonedust on the wind,

Why not hearth-strings, too,
And eye-sworn pledges—
The clockwork of the heart?

And all those frantic pauses
In the rush of mind —
The little absolutes that blind —
Can we trap and carbon-date our thoughts?

The seed that steals from yesterday
Arrests and makes of time a fool;
Unlike the mind, the acorn is a time-trap
That never went to school.

ABSENT MIND

his absent mind at play
in worlds that old men never know
refuses to return
to wars, and gods, and blood—
to true believer causes warranted
to lead to universal brotherhood.

beyond that rim of inner light
where good folk never stray,
the poet and his absent mind
indulge in pristine absent play—

where butterflies with spiders dance
there's little chance
for human webs to trap his mind
in platitudes to save his kind.

he sees atoms burst,
moon-satellites invite a road
to half-desired, hot extinction
and in this noonday night
the poet's absent mind creates
his own fragile rim of inner light.

SPUN IN SPACE

dialogs between IS and PERHAPS
annihilate our fragmentary lives,
dusted on tomorrows
like fleeting fertilities of Nile-Silt:
Tiger, Lamb, and Sphinx disintegrate
on cosmic altars spun in space.

with blood-rent thoughts,
unbound, Prometheus slew
the gnawing vultures;
unbound, our superman
devised radioactive fission—
a new debate between PERHAPS and IS.

FLIGHT OF MIND

Beneath the pyramids are tombs,
An early testament of vanity —
Beyond the sun are other stars,
More recent testament to sanity.

From tombs to stars
Requires light —
A flight
Of mind on energy
That molecules and brain
Excite.

SAVAGE GUTTURALS

From savage gutturals
Invented into alphabets
And algebraic symbols
(The square of c times m)
We grew cunning mushrooms,
And caught the energy of suns.
We forgot:
Mushrooms grow best
In manure.

UNSPLICED NERVES

I used to bounce a thought in mind
Like wind-whipped red balloons,
Or light from mirrors tilted
During sun-filled noons.

So much of every spring
Works in absorbing shock,
In leaping over unspliced gaps
Of countless splintered nerves,
That leaping thoughts and I agree:
One-way, inner destination must suffice.

We say:
Reflection is the play
Of angles lost to prisms
With the gift of rainbows,
Lost to that lens which sharpens
Pyramids of wanton images
That every light-bend knows.

HOT ATOMIC PARTS

When men explode their worlds
Into my prophetic fears,
Will any nailed, bleeding hands
Emerge to understand my tears?
What primal magic can the poet choose
To recombine those hot atomic parts
Sent hurtling into space by mindless hearts?

THE MIND OF TIME

Add space to time
to get events,
to points add instants
to create a moment.
Take heart from mind
to freeze a word,
and thought from love
to loosen limbic rut.
To life add death
for immortality —
point-instants drifting
on the mind of time
beyond the heart's mortality.

WHEN STARS LIGHT UP

the pistons of my mind know pressure
quite beyond the scope of steel:
when thoughts explode,
they move the lives of centuries
and make tamed matter reel.

it isn't stars light up,
it's we go out;
it isn't god who steers,
but mind,
about the business of our fears.

FREEDOM TO CONFORM

from Africa through India to Japan
our automated gods are Gothic
backdrops for gnawing discontent

today's corn rituals have a cast
grimmer than Mayan blood rites—
unnumbered worshipers
demand their daily bread
and freedom to conform,
but nothing for the head

YESTERDAY'S EUMENIDES

in fierce silences
my voice,
like piercing quiet after dying,
or fission in eastern cemeteries,
proclaims the day
to spite the death.
it is the unheeded shriek
of yesterday's eumenides—
forgotten vengeances
of half-forgotten gods—
hopelessly asserting beauty
in a chain-reacting cloud
of human
dust.

A NOBLER BREED

Are we no nearer Man
Than when our Quest began?
Does anyone concede
That ours is not a nobler breed
Because we built smart machines
And probed the mystery of genes?
Though we know the stars are fire
And atoms now require
Chains to tame the suns,
Nations flout international laws,
Children still inherit tragic flaws
Of bigotry, and their first toys
Are guns.

WHEN MANKIND DIED

I was there —
atomic ashes on atomic bones —
when mankind died:
pushbutton corpses —
blind mouths worshiping
 nuclear high command —
 scientists of Babel,
  fragmented global
        band,
        procl
        aiming
        archaic
        rituals
        in a
        dying
        land

II
DANCING OUT OF PHASE

INCOHERENT FLESH

a thought can be a bullet from the brain
shot outward toward a desperate goal,
or it can be a piece of steel that rips a hole
in incoherent flesh that's lost the will to feel.

step by easy step,
the mind slips down
to cellars lit by sunless days
stored with short-cut thoughts
to lunar phantoms
dancing out of phase—
until it rested on the frown
that happy madness wears.

BEYOND THE SCOPE OF STEEL

my sanity sits upon a rim of alcohol
tempting a cowering ego to grow tall,
to stretch, explode into the sun
to burn away what infancy had spun.

the pistons of my mind know pressure
quite beyond the scope of steel:
when thoughts explode,
they move the lives of centuries
and make tamed matter reel.

GARBLED DAY

no gentle night
can quite remove
the garbled day—

no May
entirely erases
all December's traces—

no shock,
however electric, therapeutic,
removes that inner rim of light
that puts on brain a lock
to keep December and the garbled day
beyond coherent sight.

THE MIND'S SCALE

The inner balance of the mind,
Too finely scaled,
Cannot decide a weight—
But measures pain
And unborn smiles.

To test it:
Just drop a thought
Upon that tilted inner pan
To set the balance right,
Then scan the silent arcs:

The sharpest pointer cannot gauge
The mass that separates the tallest ache
From thoughts that cower, first, then rage
Against the black, unmeasured night.

SUPEREGO

What tyrant whips blood scars on the inner mind,
Belated payments for a guilt grown blind?
Which hell-ring must the routed ego seek
In search of temporary sanity—
Compensation for illusions of fleshly vanity?
When elbows, knees, and trembling fingers
Ask their hearing,
The final level of denial
Spins immortality from death
And moistens cold mirrors with no breath.

WHEN NO ONE HEARS

are you there?
though smiling, your
face failed to invite mind,
to understand and measure
thought —
when no one hears
no light of satisfaction comes
from whispering obscenities
at the night
what light remains
between these poles
dims with dawn
only to profit hungry druggists

STRAIGHTJACKET

When earthworms fly,
And larks in burrows nest,
When dry brains taste drumbeats
And watches are irrelevant to time,
The suffocating mind will grasp
That nothing satisfies a straightjacket
Except the happy frown
That madness wears.

SANITY'S ONE-SIDED

I used to think
there were two sides to sanity,
theirs and (of course) mine,
with all else caught between—
poets know exactly what I mean.

Why, any child knows
that pumpkins make fine carriages
that princes who marry paupers
alone know ideal marriages;
yet grownups always laugh
at children stretching tall on tiptoes
after real or non-existent rainbows.

When I see children so derided,
I know that sanity's one-sided:
it's they who walk outside the rim
while I (of course) am safe within.

I PLAY WITH SANITY

A child with lettered blocks,
Toy soldiers, and a one-eyed doll,
I play with sanity:
Incredible languages emerge—
Fantastic, plastic wars without a dirge,
A mushroom blindness
Hotter than the sun—
Patterns only I recall
Become hot keys to inner locks
From which most people
Have always run.

MADNESS IS THE HOPE

Madness is the hope
Confusion seeks in inner order —
Structured by desperate mind —
Errant visions
Our outer patterns
Cannot see, or feel, or find.

I'VE MET WITH MADNESS

The blinding blaze of inner noon
Knows chaos caught within a little room
Reserved for gods, witches, and other
Absolutes
Devised to prison all the roots
That trees of knowledge send
Beyond the final end.

I've met with madness more than once,
Then killed it with a rhyme
Contrived in madness out of time.

III
DISTILL THE HEART

I HEARD A FLY

I heard a fly
crawl up the wall,
and dust, like pebbles
pelleted the windowsill.
a steamdrop
screamed down the windowpane,
three shadows shivered in the corner,
waiting for the sunlight
to shout them into white obscurity.

how loudly life insinuates itself
into the shuttered chambers of my ear,
and all because a tear
dropped with dreadful
plash
upon my
pill
ow.

DISTILL THE HEART

Distill the heart into a chemist's flask,
Heat, filter, purify, and collect it,
And still each lover's trembling lips will ask,
"Please, sir, what is it you've detected?"

LIDS UNLOCK

the moment just before
drooping lids unlock the inner mind
is like a dying hearth —
hot shadows hide-and-seek
to disappear in glowing embers
we have spilled across our fears

LOVE IS A LEAPING TOY

Love is a leaping toy,
A jack-in-box
That children see as joy.
To old men it's a tired plaything,
A means, perhaps, to some end or other.
It's eternity to bad poets
And, alas, to women, it means Mother.

What ruffled feathers
Think beyond in-heat display?
What Romeo hears
Beyond the nightingale, to day?
Does any heart in feverish beat
Remember, after, to retreat?

When all his pyramids at last decay,
What vain hope then does the child obey?

THE POET'S MIND WILL STOOP

If love's doors aren't ajar,
The poet's mind will stoop to keyholes
To see beyond the heart's mask
The soft lights, the hard flask —
To see what lovers are,
When naked passion shouts
And eager beasts assume
domesticated roles.

ALL FEELING ERECT

Like silence
into music—
or darkness
into slivered sunrays—
or numbness leaping to life,
all feeling erect—

you come
unsettled
into my silence.

Like a primitive fern
I uncurl too fast
to reach for sunlight
and you smile:
"Kook!"

A VOICE THAT KNOWS STARS

I fought interruptions,
dullness and sleep.
Dead center inertia.
And then your call—
brief moments
within some medical crisis.
Suddenly my night was full—
you were part of
tomorrow.

As sea-tides
casually touch hot bayous
hidden from the gulf,
so, too, a voice that knows stars
and painted roses—
ours.

TALL, LIKE STEEL
(Rose)

I met a sailor from New Orleans,
Tall, like steel,
The only seaman
Could make me really feel.

Like a sculptured yawl,
Its curved keel true and right,
He's the only sailor
Made me sail all night.

The main mast's far aft,
Tall, with rigging tight,
This yawl was built for sailing
Through the wettest, roughest night.

But yawls and sailors leave the shore,
And he was true to kind,
Leaving a tall and billowing mainsail
Whipping through the memories
of my mind.

USELESS PANTOMIME

No matter how we love, our roses die,
Their song eludes the most remembering heart,
Their color, like the blush when suns depart,
Escapes the brightest, most retentive eye;
Soft winds will rob them of their scent, then fly
To secret caves a quiet world apart
From cities' soot and smog and frantic mart,
To keep for future blooms that dying sigh.
No mind can play the puppeteer with time,
Which pulls the cords that make our roses leap
Or droop in heaps like grave-mounds, half-alive;
No heart, however full its song, can drive
Away those winds or stop the hungry sleep
That makes of memory cheerless pantomime.

SLIVERED LIGHT

Dear Mary:
Can Indian Paintbrush or Yellow Stargrass —
Shouting colors prisoned on a quiet page
Abate the constant, cutting pains
That crowd, like raging Lears,
The center of our inner stage?

Fragile Mary:
Can tearless words, caught like slivered light
Upon the night-pools of our darker mind,
Reflect the wordless terror
Etched in scars upon your fragile bones
Which no balm seems to find?

Gentle Mary:
Can paper symphonies, a frozen *Pathétique*,
Photos of a meadowlark in flight,
Or sighs, like winds through prairie grass,
Command our soundless mind at last to hear,
And all our weighted footsteps to be light?

Courageous Mary:
The gulf between the mind and outer light
Is greater than the gasp
That separates the eye from glass —
A kind of frozen poetry that no philosophy's
Accumulated wisdom can surpass.

Dear sister Mary:
Let mind join fingertips to thought,
Distant stars and mountains to the brain,
And force my gnawing inner rage
To march, obedient, on this, my silent page.

NOT IN VERONA

centuries of words
mountains of marble
infinity of canvasses—
desperately devoted
to love:

somewhere there must be a song
nightingales and daffodils don't sing—
somewhere there must be no roses,
no moons, or shadowed trysts with lips—
somewhere there must be a sleep with no bed,
a heart with no ties to a cobwebbed head.
somewhere.
but not in Verona

PAST CATEGORIES AND TAXONOMIES

If you should find a thought
That flirts with time,
First tie it to a page
Then thrust it through your mind—
Past categories and taxonomies.
Let it grow and age.
With luck you may distill
A dram of champagne for the heart,
With bubbles for eternity
And half a new thought
Born of art.

RUSH INTO SPRING

Like rosebuds opening
To touch sunlight,
Or eager crocuses pushing
Through March snow.
I'd rush into spring —
If I were young

MAGIC JACK

The screaming ripped the air
And knives cut at my heart
As Carolyn came running in,
Cradling Patrick's little head.
I saw the blood, my bones turned cold
Instantly.
Waiters brought towels and ice,
Larry shoved us into the car
And we raced to the hospital.
   We raced, we wondered, we worried.
Comforted by his mom,
Patrick, now strangely silent,
Closed his eyes as if to sleep.
Fearing concussion, we talked him awake,
Till x-rays could search for inner damage.
At last the hospital — friendly, open,
Like hope untied to desperate promise,
Embraced us.
   Our long wait was rewarded
When Carolyn returned from x-ray.
White-clad attendants wheeled Patrick in—
Pale, the red gash on his forehead

Dominant, assertive, demanding.
"No concussion," she said.
In that little room, relief was palpable,
As if stray sunshine had dispatched the fog
Clouding our morning.
   As the surgeon readied Patrick
For the stitching, I held my breath —
And Patrick's tiny, trusting hand.
The wide, startled eyes turned to me,
An almost-smile appearing as he said,
"Tell me *Jack and the Beanstalk.*"
Though nervous laughter touched the room,
The voice, the words, the look
Shook me, held me fast,
Forever etched in mind.
Trembling inside, knees questionable,
I stole a quick breath and began:
"Once upon a time, in a land far, far away, . . ."
I felt an almost imperceptible squeeze,
As the surgeon's needle pierced flesh
And the stitching began.
   With Jack we sold the cow,
Claimed the magic beans,
Climbed the magic stalk,
Faced the thundering giant —
Patrick, Carolyn, I, and the surgeon,
Till stitching was complete.
   Protective bandage now in place,
The startled eyes relaxed, lit up,
A cautious smile appeared,
As if Jack and the wondrous beans
With magic once-upon-a-time
Had finally touched the tear-stained face.

NO PRIVATES
(For Thomas)

Were you four?
and I at 60-something?
How we walked—
so grown-up like—
hand in hand,
past fire-anthills
and cacti scattered
furtively among the trees.
Do you remember now
that secret path
you discovered
slivering through post oaks
in Carter Park?
And that ugly emasculated bronze
memorial to a Texas pioneer?
Do you remember
how indignantly you exclaimed,
"He has no privates!"
And do you remember the following year,
driving past that euphemistic horror,
still pointing, still shouting in dismay,
"Mom! There's that man with no privates!"

IV
CITY PULSEBEAT

I
NOON

choking inescapable and rapid
pulsebeat of time

PEOPLE

red black white and slightly
amber
male female gay and unisexual
visible and invisible minorities
aliens unseen unknown to
authorities
rushing crushing gushing
demanding

E X P A N D I N G

charging rushing racing
trucks minivans and long
suburbans
18-wheelers squealers
spitting fuming exhausting

long fat buses trains
and trolleys
hauling people suspended
in space and time
RACE TIME

one dead steeple

glass steel and concrete
buildings
concrete canyons dirty alleys
hot jammed streets
mechanized and choked
with people
multiplying creatures
of god

"Where is the richblack sod?"

PEOPLE

jammed freeways
chromed and plastic cars
blaring stinking honking
grinding gears
cusses traffic fears
indigestion hypertension
"Where'd ya learn ta drive, mister?"
"Up yours, sister!"
(digitally enhanced)

PEOPLE

stray dogs cats rats
homeless stray people
cops on foot on horse in squad cars
all with guns and rubber bullets
and a prod that stuns
"Don't Park. Don't Stop. Don't Stand."
DON'T
sunbaked concrete walks
pantomime on hot cement
black-hot tar-road into which
a heel will stick will stick

anemic flick of last night's neon sign
seems sick seems sick seems sick

PEOPLE

noon walk noon talk
wiggling miss and ogling guys
burgers onions grease french fries

"Grace dies."

p e o p l e p e o p l e p e o p l e

multiplying onrushing hiss
high noon's gossip-mass
"Nice ass"
bright new store
in the sterile fluorescent
in the coldly incandescent
shopping malls stuffed

PEOPLE

mass production technological seduction
gadgets and time-saving articles
dacron-orlon-wool-and-nylon
plastic totally synthetic
steel-and-concrete cradle of today
the only way
to raise the living standard
and sell soap

choking inescapable and rapid
buoyant exhilarating vapid
madrushing pulsebeat of SPACETIME

II
NIGHT

wet red neon-night
drops of crimson light
delight the hungry eye
tall heels click
on the slick walk
and people talk shop
block after block

bright wet neon-night
bloodred signs entice
the eager eye:
BUY!
pizza beer trusses
hamburgers onions grease
hotdogs chickenfried steak
bras shoes luxury spectacles
exlax beer and booze
perspiration constipation
CHOOSE! compare
beware
cars cabs bikes trucks buses
impatiently beep creep
blink and shout ("Jeese!")
("Doesn't anyone sleep?")
metal wheels on metal track
make metallic music
screak crack trolley-clang
stuffed with people to the back
subway trains and buses
eject their sardine patrons
little girls with painted faces
juveniles in too-tight levis
hot eager men and stylish matrons

hot, red neon-night!
winking signs invite
the anxious eye:
SUPERCOLOSSAL! STUPENDOUS!
marquees blink beckon blink
beckon-and-blink
Cinerama Imax and Three-Dee
superdigital DTS stereo and directional
sound can be objectionable
beckon-and-blink
fastfood cigarettes and MIXED DRINK
cigars cigarettes (KING SIZE)
nicotine and mixed drink
only man is able to devise

CITY NIGHT !
alive and calculated
to incite:
jukebox jungle boogy-beat
traps the feet and dulls the mind
to rhythmical submission
Late Edition!
murder rape
to rhythmical submission
AIDS
anthrax missiles fusion fission
international nuclear confrontation
("Mushrooms grow best in manure")
No Escape
don't stop don't park don't stand
don't loiter don't walk
DON'T!
whistle-cop
redgreenandamber STOP
firesirens' ambulances' wail
escalate aggravate

irritate
grate

winking-red city-night!
alive alight and calculated –
to excite delight invite incite
tall heels click
on the slick pavement walk
and night creatures talk shop
block after block

III
MIDNIGHT TO THREE

fewer marquees blink

dim-fronted theaters
expel their squinting patrons
reluctant middle-aged matrons
girlishly giggling
wiggling
loudly announcing cocktails
at dimly lighted places
eccentric egocentric
levi-centric twilight creatures,
reluctantly emerging out of action features
escape down dim and beckoning sidestreets
down alleys jammed
with the foolish and the damned
sugardads and pretties
roam the city's hungry streets
tired and indifferent cops
with clubs and guns
patrol or half-patrol their beats
misdirected youth

beautiful uncouth
drift from dive to dive
swilling and gin-milling
into desperate security

mainstreet slowly dies
furtive eyes suck life
from stragglers passing by
all sexes on the make
escaping social hexes
seek and roughly take

animal starvation:
innocents in search of drugs
and defiant diversion
drink the last few dregs
of night's perversion
stimulate simulate fornicate

no marquees blink

IV
JUST BEFORE DAWN

hungry streets

papers dust beercans
leftovers
from night's frantic fuss
whirled by every feeble gust
or car-exhaust

homeless huddled
in dark corners
or on hot-air grates

a derelict drags
a stooped and tattered frame
to rest

bleary-eyed Don-Juans
frustrated dissipated loneliness
sits on all-night stools
in hamburger and fastfood places
(grease onions french fries)
taut and tired faces
fixed and vacant eyes

DEBRIS

a street-cleaning crew
with whirring dust brushes
patronless begging cab or two
half-painted prostitute coffee bound
occasional speeding car
wayward bus
creaking emptily ahead of schedule

DEBRIS

beercans
dust
hustlers huddled in doorways
"Got a buck mister?"
furtive eyes search
other furtive eyes
for recognition and connection
guardedly present erection

a pigeon or starling
stealing last night's crumbs
in front of deserted night clubs

from deserted bums
a worn-out waitress
gay guys arm in arm
a lone gray man sits
closed eyes bowed head
on a park bench
NO PARKING
whirling dust paper
beercans

DEBRIS

hungry streets await
the first gray light
the early worker's yawn
and other harbingers of hot day's fight
the inescapable and rapid
city pulsebeat in SPACETIME

V
FOOTSTEPS ON WATER

DAYS RUN

Like little ripples
ever outward,
some sunlit
some in shadows lost,
my days run,
then into incoherence
break.

I skip
another stone
to make the ripples
run.

PAST OURSELVES

Each dawn
I part the morning fog
And court the sun—
But we remain strangers,
Glaring past our selves
To rims that bind the universe,
Its crabs, giants, dwarfs,
But not our light.

PEPPERMINT POLES

Fragments jump out —
As peppermint poles
In Christmas windows shout,
And hope routs fears,
As fragile snowflakes
Endlessly flurrying, hurrying,
Shatter fragile beauty
On indifferent frozen lakes.
In this winter world
I build brave crystal castles
In a peppermint-painted land,
Aloof, but still a part,
And built by trembling hand.

ANIMALS INTRUDE

Like hope upon a fragile rainbow
Or light upon the edge of day —
Outstretched, the invitation lay,
Till animals intrude
And laugh the pain away.

HOUSMAN TO EMILY

As Housman is to Emily,
So are you to me:
You store the fear within,
I expand in happy agony.

You must be peremptory,
I, vitally oblique;
You kissed your hand to me and died,
Indifferent whether missed,
Or whether our two hearts had lied.

FOOTSTEPS ON WATER

Like footsteps on water,
Or shadows when the sun dies,
We move across seamless days,
Shouting ME and I
And beauty at the wind —
Beauty at the wind —
Beauty at —

TOO SUBTLE FOR THE KNIFE

In March there are spring days
When truth hides in bouquets,
Too subtle for the knife,
Eloquently elusive of the life
Which only roses know—
And so incredibly below
A man not even microscopes
Can find that ultimate degree of mind
Which love and beauty court
And our stars and sun support.

SPARKS UPON A PAPER SHELF

I fault you less
Than blame myself
For storing futile sparks
Upon a paper shelf.

Now yesterday is ashes,
Tomorrow — smoke and dust —
And well-oiled friendship wheels
Grind uselessly to rust.

This restless rage within
Immobilizes thought,
Like wind and winter freeze,
Inexorably creeping forward
To still our northern seas —
As if some god had pulled a plug
To drop the sky before me
To kill a struggling bug.

FLIGHT SO UNLIKE BIRDS

meeting me in flight
so unlike birds
is hazardous — I know —
it happens on most days
oftener at night

yesterday,
halfway to coffee break,
a piece of colored sun
caught my glasses
and I was jetisoned off —

you should've seen me soar —
through the plate glass door,
up, across glazed tiles
and onto cabinet files —
refracted, unshattered,
precisely at — LOFF

sunlit

STRETCHING

The morning danced into my mind
As unobtrusively as rainbows onto mist,
Or shadows sharpened by a sudden noon.
Today will be alive, I thought,
Stretching into movement.

CEREBRAL STOREHOUSES

the mind projects the heart
into tomorrow
how else can a cry survive
the last echo?
or the rainbow in a tear
distill a sorrow?
how long —
without cerebral storehouses,
without libraries,
without children's memories,
without the play, the song, the word —
how long can hot erections —
monuments to heroic passion —
endure?

HOPE IS A HAGGARD JADE

Hope is a haggard jade,
peering through windows
at other lives on parade:

"An array of wooden moments"
she scowls; "an endless string
of no tomorrows
made ludicrous by yesterday's sorrows."

In reply, the world howls.
The hag snaps shutter and shade:
"The piper hasn't paid,"
she growls.

WHEN THE BUTTERFLY REMEMBERS

When the butterfly remembers
his cocoon
and night recalls the noon,
when old men seek the womb
and Hemingways their tomb,
no wonder then
intelligence admits the loon,
the piper pays
and dancers call the tune.

NO SILENCE STEPS

no silence steps
so strong as hidden love
in tired hearts
alive with memory's song

no May can dance for June,
no sunlight mourn for snow –
it is a secret tune
that makes our ashen embers
glow

SECRET SPRINGS

however sharp
it makes the heart,
love dulls the wit
and films the eyes
with promises
of happy coexistence

however full the mind,
it never seems to find
the secret springs
of childhood's bold resistance
fraternity is still a child
crying after games,
the holy names
fragmented into fears
by too many creeping years

LIDS UNLOCK

the moment just before
drooping lids unlock the inner mind
is like a dying hearth —
hot shadows hide-and-seek
to disappear in glowing embers
we have spilled across our fears

I turn to reach the
phantom shadows dancing
out of time and space
but cannot touch your face

heavy lids unlock tomorrow
and hot shadows dance
in a forbidden place

SYLPHS

like half-remembered sirens
tempting sunshine
into Sunday morning shadows,
fantastic sylphs
in Chopin pirouettes
spin across the carpet
of my mind:
sound into sight,
spinning bursts
of free passion.

yesterday
these whirls were spun
by some frantic thought

within a heart,
to burst into ephemeral flight
today.

with half a sigh
sylphs and sirens die,
fragments
scattered in the cellars
of my half-awakened mind.

good morning
I didn't hear you knock

SHADOW AND SUBSTANCE

anticipating sound
where distant echoes played,
confusing shadow with substance,
was with is,
pattern with puppet,
teeth with smile,
she waited.

the dance was empty,
the breasts cold,
head games old—

thanks for dinner
of course I love you!
same time next week?

A HOLE IN TIME
(For Allen)

Grief rips a hole in time -
It is a shouting silence
That overpowers reason,
Claws the heart into shreds
Then, reluctantly, perches on memory
Like a burning, crimson sunset
Turning long shadows into yesterday
But still promising tomorrow.

A TOUCH OF MIND

no day contains the mind,
no tear the heart—
within the compass
of the tightest thought
our universes drift apart

to grasp a hand takes faith
to touch a heart, the inner eye,
and thought must meet with thought
before two minds enclose a sigh

nor fingertips nor parted lips
can match a touch of mind,
that unslaked inner fire—
like sparks from steel
or hope astride despair—
ignites recalcitrant realities
and builds real castles
in imaginary air.

VITA
(For Harriette)

Caught in a sea of conflicted emotions,
Wave-tossed, directionless, and self-indulgent,
Gasping for breath, for life postponed
By fantasies denied,
In rage my soul protests, "No more!"
Till in that sea of half-invited pain,
Waves of discontent and raw anxiety
Purge, at last, the spleen inhibiting my brain
From measured action.

Now in my backyard tree a bird sings,
The August wind reminds me that this day's alive
With sunshine. I hold this living warmth
Firmly, and shout "Vita! Vita!"
See? There she comes.

LOUISA'S

At the Pink Elephant they said
"Go down to the ship channel,
To Louisa's." They promised
Greek sailors dancing arm in arm.

Downtown Houston's lights
Seemed like distant bright scars
Against the night sky
As we walked the wet streets
To find Louisa's.
And the sailors.

Suddenly we were there:
A combination of laughter and light
Punctuated the humid air.

Packed wall to wall,
The place smelled beer, fish,
Smoke, and sweat.
A jukebox blared Greek music
For the sailors, circling arm in arm.

But the Greek sailors do not really dance.
They imitate half-remembered ritual beats,
And, like Narcissus, hear their leaps
Imaged in a circle of liquid applause,
As mirrors lose their images
When lights go out.

When lights go out,
What hot rhythm darkness hides, I know,
Between the sailors row on row.

BEYOND THE EDGE

Travel through the heart,
Astride a tear or not,
And hear, as dolphins do,
The songs your ears do not.
Touch words that hang
Too warmly on the softest lips —
Explore pastels with fingertips
That see beyond the eye.

Taste honey-wine that can't be bought
And lust can never brew;
Conjure up the sweetness of the rose
That Juliet and Romeo knew;
Then ask of reason if it understands
The tears, songs, and heat,
The half-formed kisses out of mind
Beyond the edge of thought.

MARKING TIME

"Is that all?"
I asked the cacophonous bird?
"To lose our voices on the wind?"
"Is there no way
To make our mark indelible—
Like mountains, or the sea?"
But all he did was scream.

"Is there no way," I persisted,
"To be unique and known,
Not just another vegetable
Grown for time's appetite?"

He puffed his feathers —
Blue and impertinent in the sun —
Flapped a wing and tipped his head,
"Be a Jay! Be a Jay!" he said,
Then fluttered on.

THE BIRD

A fish with wings
Met a bird with scales.
"Why don't you swim?'
He asked the bird.
"Because you do not fly,"
The bird's reply.

THE ELEMENT OF DISHARMONY
(For Kelley)

I build bridges people cross
To other shores,
I kindle fires and desires
Others burn,
I am the means to ends
That others seek,
The seed that men in others plant,
The sanity in rant
And in the orthodox the cant.
I am the tool
That cut design in chaos
And in form the element of disharmony.
To death I'm sometimes life
And with no breath
I move future air—
Now . . . now . . .
As I reach for Kansas.

MORNING MASS

To pluck a star
Needs but a wink
And shadows
On the edge of light
Where feelings are—
Where in the morning grass
The night, retreating,
Dances diamonds,
Caught on morning rosaries
To say at morning mass.

SHREDDED SAILS

The way the Indian sits
On nails,
And Mayas bled before
Their Sun—
The way my fragile boat
With shredded sails slips
Into hungry waves—
I practice continence.

VI
AFRICAN GENESIS

RAMPANT GENES

To feel a star that warms the eye
Needs only simple life,
The frail commodity
That universal shops display
For rampant genes to buy.

And yet between our mind and light
The gulf is greater than the gasp
That separates the eye from glass—
A kind of fixed and sunless wisdom
That poets sometimes can surpass.

AFRICAN GENESIS

You think in blood and call it game,
You know the glassy eye you will not see,
You know when short hair stands,
You know the flared nostrils
And the clammy hands,
But do you wonder, Why?
Young hunter, teach me why
I cannot love a gun
Or want a frantic heart to die.

Imprisoned in the freedoms others forged,
You laugh in lies
And speak your words from other mouths.
Swinging from ancient tree-limbs
Rooted in your heart,
Teach me, young hunter,
The beast that can't be learned,
The pattern of archaic kill,
This virgin rage politely turned.

THE HAMSTER AND THE RAT

The hamster and the rat proclaim
That all my treadmills have been set
Irrevocably
In genetic and in social time—
As if my voiceless thoughts,
Imprisoned in the attics of my mind,
Were unnatural, perpetrated crime,
Unconnected and irrelevant
To the atom's energetic fission.

Beyond the radioactive isotopes
On which my neighbors hang their hopes
The urgent question stays:
Will children last beyond that nuclear winter
That turns our years to days?

PROMISE AT DAWN

In wild dawn flight
From sunrays
And civilization,
A trembling wide-eyed faun
Paused before a misted pool
Of quiet promise.

Proud and fragile flower,
Like rooted butterflies before the wind,
Shatters when the ardent executioner obtrudes.
A shot explodes
The promise at dawn.

DAWN DENIES THE LARK

Each night revives
The promise each day offers:
Concrete obelisks and crossed spires,
Like mushrooms in manure,
Promise easy resurrections.
Words, like children's toys
Arrayed in tinny rows,
Heroic in their tinny creeds:
Quixote is Hamlet,
Ulysses in Hitler's guise
Invents a democratic horse;
Crude jingles rival Milton,
Plato instructs Socrates in the hemlock art,
Odes and easy fictions chain the moon to love,
An uneasy pen anticipates the promised sunrise.

Each day becomes a tomb
For every night's design
Which bows to hunger and to thin purses.

Every dawn denies the lark
Our infant dreams.

FLOWERS KNOW

There are pressures
Only flowers know—
Heat divorced from suns,
Tension of tender buds afraid
To split green shells—
Or, perhaps, in natural wisdom,
The pregnancy of promise,

A bursting color
That looks for marriage
With a windblown thought
That bees cannot avoid.
Perhaps.
The pregnant bluebonnet knows
How children drift
Like dust through timeless trees:
The tamest seventeen
Is heat and thoughtless wind and bees,
Like waves that never heard of seas.

RITUAL DANCE

Who can understand
this daily waggle dance?
For bees it points
to sweeter paths
for kin to follow.

Your higher code,
traced automatically,
must intervene
(you say) between
my feeling flesh
and daily ritual dance,
to forestall
(you say) that final fall

Don't you know
the dance is all?

THE LIMBIC LOBE

Below the mind
Squats the limbic lobe,
Where rage, hunger, lust
Shout obscenities
At measured sanity.
Primitive, inarticulate,
Archaic and absolute,
It sits in judgement on civility:
A sense of biologic revelation.
Above the hungry grasp of limbic urge
Lives a dream to build monuments—
An ephemeral thought
Stretching past hot concrete
To hills and rainforests.

Beyond that aching dream
No raging limbic urge will serve
The glassy chill of dying nerve.

FIG LEAVES

ape and nightingale
are kin,
gained feathers
through original sin,
eating apples of knowledge
no college
can provide

a nightingale eats
forbidden worms
(not fruit)
and ape is man—
enough to be a brute

NO DECEMBER

each midnight steals
from noon,
December robs the spring

time and August see
but thistles on the wind
and half a dying rose—

it is the acorn knows
no December,
no joke of immortality,
and quietly awaits the oak.

ROOTED FREEDOM

Confined in space
We run, or streak in hot steel
Across paved roads to escape our prisons.

Like proud eagles
We too must leave our sunfilled clouds
To perch on the ever-tightening rim of night.

As settled oaks know silent flight
Leaf, branch, and trunk stretching for the sun,
We too obediently search out our rooted freedom.

UNROOTED THOUGHT

Thought is irrelevant to noise
Unless it court that incoherence
Only screech-owls and hyenas know.

This noise-creating techno-man man
So intent on instant and unrooted thought—
As if the smile of steel and gun
Could instantly replace the mind that makes
Both clotted blood and fixed stars run.

Through screaming jets, sirens,
And cities chained by noise-machines,
A silence prays for space in time.

COMMON WEBS

This netted universe
Imperils every poet's wingspread,
And still I'd rather try
To manage timeless flight
Clear of common webs
Than seek refuge in rooted safety.

GILL-SLITS

perched
on space-junk
tied
to space-junk
with time's umbilicals,
we ride the solar wind
across the moon-curved rim of earth,
auto-pilot scream-monitored,
then parachute into seas
to bob among bewildered fish—
still tied to our own gill-slits.

NATURE'S CALL

Assured and proud stood man,
With acorn and with cone,
Declaiming on his obvious Plan:
"Did ever acorn grow to pine?
There is a strategy to life
That forces Who to every tongue,
As if demanding to be known."
And every mother-listener's wife
Nodded to her Sunday young
And confidently sang *"Amen."*
Towering, tongueless, far above,
The oak, stirred by the wind,
In anger whispered, What?
And from the shadows caught
Within its branches came
Nature's call: Who? Who?
As if the question were
Imprisoned by the word—
As green light is by *green.*

NAMELESS CREATURES

When Moses let man
Invent the names
That label life,
He set mind
Against its self—
To putting endless tags
On endless bottles
On an endless shelf.

Nameless creatures
Don't wait for labels
Before they eat of life.

UNLIKE OTHER CREATURES

"Are ants, bees, and sponges
Socially aware?" I asked.
"Do snakes and toads communicate,
Programmed by genes
To be mere food machines?
Alive, alert, and keen,
Do tigers know themselves,
Or are they just genetically mechanic?
Do upright anthropoids
Know self and that they'll die?
If men barbecue bloody flesh
For sport and appetite,
And know — and fear — the worm,
Why not jackals and wolves,
Or even garbage rats?"
"You are a fool, my son,"
A brother rat replied;
"We're not like other creatures.
For us, tomorrow always comes."

UNBUTTON TIME

Unbutton time,
Relinquish space,
Till mind seek metaphor
Instead of place.

MIND ESCAPE

The worm is ignorant of sky
unless it knows the butterfly—
as man, in search of mind escape,
must seek in upright hominids
the posture of the swinging ape.

BIOLOGY IS FULL OF JOKES

night is a place where children
dream of growing up
and older folks of being young—
biology is full of jokes:
December longs for March,
the tight bud for flowers,
and in that final Drought
all demand immediate showers

TO CATCH A DAY

If you should catch a day,
First carve it —
To your own dimensions,
Make it wait obediently;
Then, quietly as moments
Poised regally for death,
Collect the debris of your mind
And sweep it —

Into poems of the marble kind.

VII
WINDOWS

GUILT

So painful was the thought
I let it drop
to marble halls
my mind had built
within the heart —
since when I've stored
so many
that the walls
have split
and freed the monster
guilt.

EMPTY CAMERA

without mind
the eye's a useless camera -
darkness pierced by light
will yield no patterned sight -
only the inner chaos
of the blind

WINDOWS

the windows of my mind
shut faster than the doors of heart -
far easier to exorcise a thought
than ban emotion at the start

YOU CANNOT ETCH A SMILE

You cannot etch a smile
on magnetized recording tape,
nor so immortalize a wink —
unless a Mozart or a Brahms
transform a kiss to melody.

music makes of silence sound
and out of sound a silence —
can Michelangelo
move sight to sound?
transmute the frescoe's eye of fear
into a panic we can hear?

HATE

Hate is like an old
    love affair —
The torch is charred
    and marble-cold,
but all the fires's there.

IRRELEVANT TO SAND

To separate the *need*
From all the *must* of obligation
Is at last to feel
One pulse of life's equations —
Not every oyster yields a pearl:
When sea's irrelevant to sand,
Your pearl is forced to grow on land

LIFT A LID

To see, you simply lift a lid
To let a thought escape —
To hear, create a sound.
To touch, you capture cats
On stretching fingertips.
To know, you measure thought
In words asleep in tired books,
Or capture distance on a page —
A page tied to poets
From a noiseless and unlidded age.

A ROSE IS NOT A NAME

dear Gertrude:
a rose is not a rose
until it joins the mind in thought—
nor bee nor butterfly can pose
the object for our inner eye—
unseen, unknown, unsought.
one learns
the rose,
sunsets and trees,
and that highway traffic flows—
then, if the patterns
tell the brain it sees,
the mind becomes aware it knows,
and happily invents the symbol *rose*.

I say:
take the rose—
red, or yellow tea,
on bushes, in vases,
even in imaginary places.

I say:
take the rose—
Juliet's or Cummings'
Gertrude Stein's, or Burns',
take them together, or in turns.

then tell me:
Did you use your nose,
or pen to grasp it?
did you use hand,
heart, or mind to clasp it?

I say:
drain your mind of words,
then inject roses—
and if your brain bleed
like your thorn-stuck thumb,
evict the mental thorns—
and stick them—
onto roses.

IS 5

I laugh at coldly pious men
and scorn their minds' retreat
before unknown arithmetic
that unborn Einsteins will complete:

it's time for mankind
to acknowledge that *Is 5*
is more than twice infinity
and considerably more alive.

SUDDENLY IT'S 40

from levis, popcorn,
and hair shorn
in crewcut fashion,
it's just three growing pains
to mellowed immaturity:

enthusiastic forenoon lights
lengthen into afternoon,
suddenly it's 40,
and you haven't had lunch!

RUE

Were I, like roses, pricked to beauty,
Or, like night-breath, crystallized to dew,
I might abandon both my lives
for rose-filled winds
And all my tears for noon's dry rue.

BLESSED ARE THE WEAK

blessed are the weak in mind
for they shall populate the earth;
more blessed are the sterile kind
for they cannot possibly give birth.

AMPLE ROOM

The mind has ample room
for mountains, seas
distant friends,
even absent sunshine
when it extends

walls.

RUSH INTO SPRING

Like rosebuds opening
To touch sunlight,
Or eager crocuses pushing
Through March snow.
I rush into spring —
As if I were young

BARS OF MIND

thought is a bird uncaged —
beyond the bars of infant mind —
flight is the test of cages —
vision — applied to the blind.

IMPRISONMENT

Imprisonment?:
Is freedom shuttered in or out?
Even dearest friends don't hear
That inner shout—fierce, stretching,
Yet to those friendly ears
Invisible as darkness is to light.
Imprisonment
Has less to do with place
Than with those mental bars
We stretch across the face.

UNPRINTED BREATH

Our thoughts are prisoned
By the arbiters between our inner chains
And printed freedoms—
Words don't bleed, weep, or explode
In liquid sound for deaf worlds to hear;
And though the formulas of craft
May sometimes free a shouting thought,
Life's sting remains stubbornly within,
Awaiting the last unprinted breath.

ETERNAL AGONISTES

Like divine illusion caught
Between the womb and dying,
Some interludes beget children,
But most intrude,
Like happiness on meditation—
Like Milton's blindness
Into the dark of noon,
The eternal agonistes
Of the thinking soul

SHATTERED GLASS

As if Prometheus
From some elemental sand
Had sculptured man in glass –
He stands,
An echo of the gods.

What secret goddess
Breathed fragile life
Into that elemental heart?

Crystal starlight shatters
At the gentlest touch,
Heaping heart-slivers
In glassy mounds to memory.

TEMPTING SUNSHINE

as polished prisms
tempt sunshine
into Sunday morning shadows,
fantastic sylphs
in Chopin pirouettes
whirl and leap across
the carpet of my mind,
sound into sight,
releasing souls
I've sheltered
through this long night—
my life.